D1824369

Draft of Laws, Constitution, Objects, &c.

Church Choir Guild Canadian Branch

BIBLIOLIFE

CANADIAN BRANCH

OF THE

CHURCH CHOIR GUILD.

(Guild of Church Musicians.)

REGISTERED.

DRAFT OF LAWS, CONSTITUTION, OBJECTS, &c.

Prepared at the request of the honourable Warden, J. H. LEWIS, Esq., Mus.D , D.C.L., by the Council in London, and confirmed at Conference, 1892.

Name.

That this Branch of the Guild be denominated " The Canadian Branch of the Church Choir Guild."

Objects.

1. The Church Choir Guild is an institution established as a means of union, and of setting forth the duties of those who devote their musical capabilities to the praise and honour of Almighty God, in beautifying the Worship of His Holy Church.

2. The advancement of Church Music by means of Lectures, Competitions, Musical Performances, an Annual Conference, Services, Organ Recitals, &c.

3. To receive Church choirs in union and provide a code of rules for their use, and to encourage meetings of combined Choirs for Festivals.

4. The granting and registration of Certificates of Proficiency to Members of Enrolled Choirs ; and the conferring of the Diplomas of Associate and Fellow (after Examination), upon Members of the Guild.

5. When possible to afford pecuniary assistance to Members of the Guild who may be in need.

6. To raise a fund for providing a Guild Hall, with Organ, Reading Room, Library, &c., for the use of Members.

7. Any other means by which Choral Worship of the Church may be improved.

Constitution.

The Guild shall consist of Members, Associates, Fellows, and Honorary Fellows.

The General Council consists of an Honorary President, Honorary Vice-Presidents, Patrons, Honorary Chaplain, Warden, Honorary Sub-Warden, Organizing Secretary, Treasurer and Registrar, Honorary Secretary, Honorary Organist, two Honorary Auditors, with not more than six elected Members.

The Executive Committee is composed of the six elected Members, together with the Warden. Sub-Warden, Organizing Secretary, Treasurer and Registrar, Honorary Chaplain, Honorary Secretary, and Honorary Organist.

Election of Office Bearers.

1. The Warden, Organizing Secretary, Treasurer, and Registrar, and two Examiners (one of whom shall be the Warden), shall be appointed by, and shall be the representative of the general Council of the Headquarters of the Guild in London, and shall hold their positions subject to good behaviour, and to the satisfaction of the general Council in London.

2. In the event of either of above Officers being incapacitated from holding office by death or disease, or should wish to resign office, it shall be lawful for the General Council of the Australasian branch to select a Member from their body to undertake the duties of that office, the name of which Member shall be sent immediately to London for consent of the Executive Committee in that city.

3. At the Annual Conference the Members of the Branch shall elect the following Officers :—Honorary President, Honorary Vice-Presidents, Honorary Chaplain, Honorary Sub-Warden, Honorary Secretary, Honorary Organist, and two Honorary Auditors ; also not more than six Members.

Duties of the Various Officers.

THE HONORARY CHAPLAIN.—The Honorary Chaplain shall intone the Guild Office at the opening and closing of all meetings of the Guild.

THE WARDEN.—The Warden shall preside at all ordinary Meetings of the Guild and of the Executive Committee. He shall sign all Certificates of Membership and Diplomas, and shall conduct at all Festivals held by the Guild.

THE HONORARY SUB-WARDEN.—The Honorary Sub-Warden shall preside at all ordinary Meetings of the Guild and of the Executive Committee in the absence of the Warden.

ORGANIZING SECRETARY, TREASURER, AND REGISTRAR.—It shall be the duties of this official to take charge of all books and money belonging to the Guild. He shall send to the Headquarters of the Guild in London a proper balance-sheet showing expenditure and income each month, on the first Monday thereof, and every quarter he shall remit a bank-draft for three fourths of all moneys in his charge and which are the property of the Headquarters of the Guild in London. One-fourth of all such moneys to be kept in the bank to meet emergencies.

2. He shall register the numbers of all Certificates and Diplomas which may be granted by the Guild, and shall send a full copy of all such registrations to the Headquarters of the Guild in London every three months.

3. He shall take charge of all Examination Papers received from London, and shall hand them to the Candidates on the day of examination. At the conclusion of such Examination he shall remit the answers of the candidates together with the report of the Examiners without delay to the Headquarters of the Guild in London. For attendance at such Examination he shall receive the fee of Three Guineas, to be paid out of the General Fund.

4. He must prepare a proper Balance-Sheet for the inspection of the Canadian Branch of the Guild each year, in July and December, a copy of which shall be printed and sent to each member of the Guild.

5. He must give up his books for inspection whenever called upon by the Honorary Auditors.

6. He shall transcribe the minutes of every meeting into a minute book, and remit a summary of the doings of the Canadian Branch to the Headquarters of the Guild in London every three months.

HONORARY SECRETARY.—It shall be the duty of the Honorary Secretary to take the minutes of any Meeting of the Guild in the absence of the Organizing Secretary, Treasurer, and Registrar, and forward same to the latter official.

HONORARY ORGANIST.—The Honorary Organist shall preside at the organ at all meetings of the Guild, and at all festivals.

HONORARY AUDITORS.—The Honorary Auditors shall audit the books of the Canadian Branch of the Guild twice in each year, namely in the first week of July, and the first week of December, and shall report thereon to the General Council of the Branch. They shall make an audit whenever called upon to do so by the General Council or Executive Committee.

The Examiners.

After examination of the Candidates, the examiners shall, without delay, deliver their report to the Organizing Secretary, Treasurer, and Registrar. For their services the Examiners shall each receive the fee of half-a-guinea from each candidate for the diploma of Associate or Fellow. Five Shillings for Examination of Choristers in the Lower Grade. Five Shillings for Examination of Choristers in the Higher Grade. Seven Shillings and sixpence for Examination of Choristers in the Higher Grade Honours. Such fees to be handed to Examiners immediately after Examination of the Candidates, by the Organizing Secretary, Treasurer, and Registrar.

Examinations.

Examinations for the diplomas of Associate and Fellow shall be held in the last week of July and January in each year.

Examinations for Choristers' Certificates shall be held in July and January each year immediately before the diploma Examinations.

All papers for such Examinations shall be received from London.

All Theoretical papers shall be returned to the Headquarters of the Guild in London immediately after such Examinations, along with report of Examiners.

Examination Fees.

(A)

The fees for the Diploma of Associate or Fellow shall be Four Guineas.

Candidates shall pay the fee of Three Guineas, one Calender Month before the date of such examination, to the Organizing Secretary, Treasurer, and Registrar.

Successful Candidates shall pay the fee of One Guinea for registration to the Registrar before receiving Diploma.

Of such fees, Two Guineas shall be forwarded to the Headquarters of the Guild in London, One Guinea shall be given to Examiners, and Registration fee of One Guinea shall become the property of the Canadian Branch of the Guild.

(B)

The fee for Examination of Choristers (Lower Grade) shall be Ten Shillings, which fee shall become the property of the Examiners.

The fee for Examination of Choristers (Higher Grade) shall be One Guinea, of which Ten Shillings shall become the property of the Examiners, and Eleven Shillings shall become the property of the Canadian Branch of the Guild.

The fee for Examination of Choristers in Higher Grade (Honours) shall be Two Guineas, of which fee, Fifteen Shillings shall become the property of the Examiners, Ten Shillings shall be remitted to the Headquarters of the Guild in London, and Seventeen Shillings shall be appropriated by the Canadian Branch of the Guild.

(C)

The fee for Registration of the Lower Grade Choristers' certificates shall be Five Shillings, of which sum Three Shillings shall be sent to the Headquarters of the Guild in London, and the remaining Two Shillings shall become the property of the Canadian Branch.

The fee for Registration of the Higher Grade and Honour Certificates shall be Ten Shillings, of which sum Five Shillings shall be sent to the Headquarters of the Guild in London, and the remaining Five Shillings shall become the property of the Canadian Branch.

Laws.

1. HEADQUARTERS.—The Headquarters of the Canadian Branch of the Guild shall be in Ontario.

2. CHOIRS IN UNION.—That any Church Choir may become enrolled in Union with the Guild on making application through the Warden or Organizing Secretary. Special forms are provided for this purpose. Annual subscription half-a-guinea (which fee will belong to the Canadian Branch of the Guild). That Choirs in Union use the Constitution, Rules, &c., provided by the Council in London. Members are entitled to wear the Badge and to obtain the loan of Banner for festivals. That Choirs in Union be empowered to make Bye-laws to suit their local requirements. That free advice be given to Choirs in Union on any musical matter. That the Warden and Musical Director of Choirs in Union endeavour to attend the Annual Conference.

3. MONEYS.—That all moneys received on behalf of the Canadian Branch shall be applied towards expenses incurred in carrying out the objects of the Guild.

4. DEBTS.—That the General Council will not be in any way responsible for debts contracted by Choirs in Union.

5. MEMBERS.—That Communicants of the Church of England (ladies and gentlemen) shall be eligible for election as Members of the Church Choir Guild, the subscription being, for life, five guineas, which sum shall be remitted to the Headquarters of the Guild in London.

6. GUILD OFFICE.—That every meeting shall open and close with the Guild Office.

7. ANNUAL SERVICE.—That the Council shall endeavour to make arrangements for an Annual Service at least once a year, and also for other services as may be found practicable.

8. NOTICES OF MOTION.—Members shall have the right of sending notices of motions to be placed on the Agenda Paper for discussion at the Annual Conference, such notices to be sent to the Council through the Warden not later than November prior to such Conference. The Council reserve to themselves the right of declining Motions they may deem inexpedient, provided the Warden and President agree.

9. ORDER.—That the Warden, or in his absence the Sub-Warden, preside at all Ordinary Meetings, and, if possible, the President, or one of the Vice-Presidents or Patrons, at the Annual Conference. The decision of the Chairman on any point of order shall be final.

10. PROXY.—It shall be lawful for any Member of the Council, being present, to hold the proxy of an absent Member, which shall be available in all questions discussed.

11. RESIGNATION.—Notices of resignation must be given in writing to the Warden or Organizing Secretary, and be accompanied by a discharge of all subscriptions due.

12. BADGES.—The Badge of the Guild must be worn round the neck, at all Meetings of the Guild, by a ribbon not less than one inch wide, and of the following colours:—For Members of Choirs in Union, a pink ribbon; for ordinary Members, a dark blue ribbon; for Associates, a light t ue ribbon; for Fellows, a crimson ribbon. The Badges of the ·. uild shall be worn on all public occasions.

13. ADDITIONS TO LAWS.—That all additions to the present laws of the Guild, which may from time to time be made and sanctioned by the General Council of the Guild in London, shall be respected by the Canadian Branch.

Members.

I. That Members be entitled to a vote on all matters discussed at Conference.

II. The privilege of taking part in the Annual Service, and of attending all Festivals.

III. That free admission be allowed Members to all Lectures, &c., of the Guild.

IV. That the Calendar be sent free to all Members.

V. That Members be allowed to compete for the Medals offered by the Guild from time to time.

CHOIRMASTERS' SECTION.

(Specially designed for Choirmasters and Precentors)

SYLLABUS OF REQUIREMENTS.

ASSOCIATESHIP (A.C.C.G.)

PAPER WORK.

Questions will be set in the following Subjects :—

(1) Voice Production and Singing—viz., Questions on Breathing, Pronunciation, Articulation, and Phrasing; (2) Structure of the Anglican Chant and Gregorian Tones; (3) Harmony (including the Dominant 7th and Inversions).

PRACTICAL.

The Candidate must be prepared (1) to sing without instrumental help a scale or arpeggio to any of the five elementary vowel sounds—viz., oo, oa, aa, ai, ee ; (2) to conduct (with baton) an ordinary Anthem ; (3) to sing at sight a given Melody with simple modulations ; (4) to satisfy the Examiners in ear tests—viz., to write down the Melody of a Chant, not heard before, which the Examiners will play or sing.

FELLOWSHIP (F.C.C.G.)

(This Diploma certifies that the recipient is a qualified Choirmaster).

PAPER WORK.

Questions will be set in the following subjects :—

(1) Voiee Production, Singing, more difficult questions on the registers, Phrasing, &c., with special reference to Boys' voices ; (2) Knowledge of Cathedral Music and History of the Anglican Service ; (3) Chanting, Knowledge of the Anglican and Gregorian Systems and the Principles of Plainsong ; (4) Method of Teaching ; (5) Harmony (in not more than four parts).

PRACTICAL.

The Candidate will be examined in (1) conducting, (2) sight-singing (G, F, and C Clefs), (3) ear-tests, all of an advance standard compared with the A.C.C.G. Examination (Choirmasters' Section).

Every Candidate must be, or become, a Member of the Guild.

In case of failure, Candidates may sit again on payment of half-fee, when they will be examined only in those subjects in which they were found below the standard.

The F.C.C.G. Gown (Choirmasters' and Precentors' Section) is of black stuff, with three velvet stripes on each sleeve, each stripe an inch wide and six inches long, pointed ends. The Hood is crimson silk or poplin, edged with white fur. The square cap is black (college shape), with crimson tassel.

Associates may wear a gown similar to the Fellows, but without the velvet stripes ; a cap with black tasssel, but no Hood.

ORGANISTS' SECTION.

(Specially designed for Organists.)

SYLLABUS OF REQUIREMENTS.

ASSOCIATESHIP (A.C.C.G).

PAPER WORK.

1. Harmony (up to 4 parts).

2. Counterpoint (up to 3 parts).

3. Easy questions on the Works of the Great Composers testing the Candidate's acquaintance with the best known Classical Compositions.

ORGAN PLAYING.

1. Performance of a Standard piece, chosen beforehand by the Candidate from the following list :—

Prelude and Fugue in C	From Eight Short	
Prelude and Fugue in D minor	Preludes and Fugues.	J. S. BACH.
Prelude and Fugue in E minor	Vol. viii.　Peters.	
Prelude in G.　Op. 37 ...　...　...　...　...		MENDELSSOHN.
Postlude in D (Novello)...　...　...　...　...		SMART.
Fugue from Sonata.　No. 2　...　...　...　...		MENDELSSOHN
Andante Piacevole in B flat	(No. 1. Set 2 of Three Short Pieces)	HOPKINS.
Andante in F　...　...　...　...　...　...		SMART.
Grand Chœur in A　...　...　...　...　...		SALOME.
Andante Pastorale ("The Shepherds' Watch") *Church Musician* Office		J. H. LEWIS.

2. Playing an Anglican Chant, or Gregorian Tone, as if accompanying the *Venite*.

3. Any of the Major or Minor Scales (from memory) on the Pedals.

FELLOWSHIP (F.C.C.G.)

(This Diploma certifies that the Recipient is a qualified Organist.)

PAPER WORK.

1. Harmony of a fairly difficult character.
2. Counterpoint up to 4 parts, with Easy Double Counterpoint invertible at the Octave.
3. History and Mechanism of the Organ.
4. Plain Song, with Melodies in Ecclesiastical Modes to harmonise.
5. Fugue, so far as the relation of subject and answer is concerned, and a knowledge of the constituent parts of a Fugue.
6. Elementary "Form," and a knowledge of the Instruments used in an Orchestra, with the manner of combining them. Questions will be asked in these subjects.

ORGAN PLAYING.

1. Performance of a Standard Classical piece, chosen beforehand by the Candidate from the following list :—

Fugue in E flat (St. Ann's Tune)	BACH.
Fugue in G minor. Vol. 2. Peters.	BACH.
Fugue in A minor. Vol. 2. Peters	BACH.
Toccata in F. Vol. 3. Peters	BACH.
Fugue in B minor. Vol. 2. Peters	BACH,
Last Movement of Sonata. No. 9 in B flat	RHEINBERGER.
Fugue in G	MENDELSSOHN.
Elegy in B flat minor (Ashdown)	SILAS.
Fugue on name of Bach. No. 6	SCHUMANN
Air and Variations in A...	HESSE.
Overture in D minor and major	SMART.
Toccata in G	DUBOIS.
Sonatas. Nos. 3 or 4	MENDELSSOHN.
Air with Variations and Final Fugato	SMART.
Prelude and Fugue in C major and minor (*Church Musician* Office).	F. J. KARN.

2. Playing an Anglican Chant or Gregorian Tone as if accompanying the *Venite*, in a key chosen by the Examiners, not to exceed a tone above or below the key the Chant is written in.
3. To play from Figured Bass.
4. Extemporization.
5. Sight Reading.

Every Candidate must be or become a Member of the Guild.

In case of failure, Candidates may sit again on the payment of half-fee, when they will be examined only in those subjects in which they were found below the standard.

The F.C.C.G. Gown, Hood and Cap (Organists' Section) are similar to those of the Choirmasters', with the addition of an Edging of Gold Shot Silk to the neckband of the Hood.

CHORISTERS' CERTIFICATES.

(LOWER GRADE.)

EXAMINERS.

Choirmasters who, having passed the Higher Grade with Honours, or an equivalent examination, and being Members, shall be appointed and removable by the Council; and who shall, when practicable, conduct the examination in presence of a Clerical President.

The examination may be taken either in the ordinary or Tonic Sol-Fa notation.

Thirty marks must be gained to secure a " Pass," and forty a " Pass with Honours," there being three classes of the latter.

Maximum, 50 Marks.

Requirements.

I.—VOICE.

To sing slowly and *mezza voce*, in the three keys given, the Tonic Chord ascending, and the scale descending, thus--*do, mi, sol, do : do, si* (or *te*), *la, sol, fa, mi, re, do,* to any convenient syllables, preferably No. 1 as above, No. 2 to *koo*, No. 3 to *lah*.

Sopranos and Tenors Keys, E♭, F, and G. Altos and Basses Keys, A♭, B♭, and C.   *5 Marks may be gained.*

II.—HYMN TUNES.

The Candidate to bring four prepared Hymns with Tunes, and sing in good time and tune, with attention to pronunciation and expression, his own part in any two verses chosen from them by the Examiner. *5 Marks.*

III.—CHANTING.

(*a*) The Candidate to sing from the pointing ordinarily in use, to a prepared chant, with good pronunciation and without hurrying, two or three verses of any Canticle chosen by the Examiner. *5 Marks.*

(*b*) Sing, as above, two or three verses chosen from the Psalter. *5 Marks.*

IV.—READING AT SIGHT.

The Candidate to sing to words, or "sol-fa," in good tune and time, the Candidate's own part in a Hymn Tune not seen before.

(*a*) If the Tune does not contain transition and half beats (or pulses)— *10 Marks.*

(*b*) A Tune containing the above— *5 Marks extra.*

V.—DICTATION AND EAR TEST.

(*a*) C being sounded as the key note, to sing three phrases of not more than five notes each, dictated by the Examiner. *5 Marks.*

(*b*) C being given as before, to tell the Examiner the names of any three notes of the scale he may sing to *lah*, or play upon a key-board not seen by you. *5 Marks.*

The names used should be those with which the Candidate is most familiar.

VI.—NOTATION.

To answer three simple questions in "Notation." *5 Marks.*

✤

REGULATIONS

FOR THE

HIGHER GRADE EXAMINATION.

HIGHER GRADE.

EXAMINERS.—**Members of the Council.**

Thirty marks must be gained in requirements 2 to 6 to secure a "Pass," and thirty additional marks in No. 7 a "Pass with Honours," qualifying to act as Choirmaster.

Maximum 100 Marks.

REQUIREMENTS.

1. Candidates must have passed the "Lower Grade with Honours."

2. VOICE CULTIVATION.—To vocalise without instrumental help, to the Italian *Ah*, two or three scales or other prepared vocal exercises, without breathiness, throatiness, or flattening; and showing good command of the "registers" of the voice.

10 Marks may be gained.

3. SOLO SINGING.—To bring three prepared Solos from Anthems or Oratorios, and sing in good Church style any of them chosen by the Examiner. *10 Marks.*

4. READING AT SIGHT.—Sing in good time and tune the Candidate's own part in any Anthem or service not seen before.

15 Marks.

5. DICTATION AND EAR TEST.—(*a*) The key-note being sounded, to sing any phrases dictated by the Examiner. *5 Marks.*

(*b*) The Tonic Chord being given, to write down the notes of the melody of a Chant not heard before, which the Examiner will sing to *lah*, or play upon a key-board not seen by the Candidate, but not more that three times. *5 Marks.*

6. CONDUCTING.—Beat the time very steadily and distinctly to any Church Composition the Examiner may choose to play or sing to your conducting, if a Choir be not available. *5 Marks*

7. HONOURS.—To write answers to ten questions upon the notation of Time, Tune, and Expression; the Minor Mode; the training of Boys' voices; and the Rudiments of Harmony.

50 Marks.

COMPETITIONS FOR 1892.

A **Silver Medal** and **one guinea** will be awarded for the best *Andante* for the organ with pedal obligato, and a **Bronze Medal** with **half-a-guinea** for the second best.

A **Bronze Medal** and **half-a-guinea** will be awarded for the best Changeable Single Chant.

A **Silver Medal** for the best Essay on the following Subject : 'The Use of Gregorian Music in the Church."

A **Bronze Medal** and **half-a-guinea** (open to Choristers of Enrolled Choirs) for the best essay on "How to Chant the Psalms."

CONDITIONS.

1. These Competitions are open to Members, Associates, and Fellows of the Guild.

2. The Council reserve the power of withholding any Prize should no Composition sent in be considered of sufficient merit.

3. MSS., having a motto or device affixed with the Composer's name and address in a Sealed Envelope bearing a corresponding mark, should be sent to Mr. J. MORTON BOYCE, F.C.C.G., with the Title in the right hand corner of wrapper, not later than Sept. 30, 1892. The report will be made known in the *Church Musician* Jan. 1893.

N.B.—**The selected** Composition in each case will become the **property** of the Guild.

(SIZE OF BADGE.)

𝕭𝖆𝖉𝖌𝖊.

ORDERS for the new Badge can now be received at the following prices :—

			£	s.	d.
18 Carat Gold	...	...	6	0	0
Silver Gilt ...	...	...	0	15	0
Silver	...	...	...	0	13	0
Bronze	...	...	0	1	6
White Metal	...	...	0	1	0

(9s. per dozen to Choirs in Union).

These Badges are most artistically designed and executed, bearing on one side the Guild insignia, and on the reverse side a beautiful sketch of three surpliced Choristers, with an Organ in the background.

Guild Office.

SANCTIONED BY THE LORD BISHOP OF LONDON.

At all Meetings of the Guild and its Council the following Office shall be said :—

(At the beginning of the Meeting.)

In the Name ✠ of the FATHER, and of the SON, and of the HOLY GHOST. Amen.

 V. Our help is in the Name of the LORD.
 R. *Who hath made heaven and earth.*
 V. Blessed be the Name of the LORD.
 R. *From this time forth for evermore.*

OUR FATHER, &c.

O LORD, let Thy blessings rest upon this Church Choir Guild. Guide all our counsels by the inspiration of Thy HOLY SPIRIT, that all we undertake may be for Thy Honour and Glory, and the good of Thy Holy Church ; through JESUS CHRIST our LORD. *Amen.*

(At the conclusion.)

Let us pray.

O LORD, we beseech Thee to accept the endeavours of Thy servants, and grant that they may be fruitful to the edification of the Church according to the fulness of Thy power ; through JESUS CHRIST our LORD. *Amen.*

The Grace of our LORD JESUS CHRIST, and the Love of God, and the Fellowship of the HOLY GHOST be with you (us) all evermore. *Amen.*

 V. Let us depart in peace.
 R. *In the Name of the Lord.*

✠

For List of Officers see Special Prospectus. Further Information may be obtained from

J. MORTON BOYCE, Esq., F.C.C.G.,

Organist of Grace Church,

Brantford,

Ontario,

Canada.

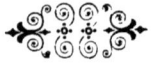

CHURCH PRINTING COMPANY, BURLEIGH STREET, STRAND, W.C.

CPSIA information can be obtained
at www.ICGtesting.com
Printed in the USA
LVIC04n0813080616
491717LV00001B/1

* 9 7 8 1 1 1 3 4 2 6 1 7 8 *